POWERPLAY
HOW TO BUILD THE PERFECT TEAM

by LINKEDIN AND TOWN HALL ACHIEVER OF THE YEAR
EY NOMINEE ENTREPRENEUR OF THE YEAR
GRAND HOMAGE LYS DIVERSITY
WORLD'S TOP100 DOCTORS

Dr. BAK NGUYEN, DMD

TO ALL THE ENTREPRENEURS, LEADERS, CHAMPIONS ,
DREAMERS AND ACHIEVERS LOOKING TO FIND A
SUSTAINABLE WAY TO SUPPORT THEIR LEGACY

by Dr. BAK NGUYEN

ISBN: 978-1-989536-50-6

ABOUT THE AUTHORS

From Canada, **Dr. BAK NGUYEN,** Nominee Ernst and Young Entrepreneur of the year, Grand Homage Lys DIVERSITY, LinkedIn & TownHall Achiever of the year and TOP 100 Doctors 2021. Dr Bak is a cosmetic dentist, CEO and founder of Mdex & Co. His company is revolutionizing the dental field. Speaker and motivator, he wrote 72 books over 36 months accumulating many world records (to be officialized).

- **ENTREPRENEURSHIP**
- **LEADERSHIP**
- **QUEST OF IDENTITY**
- **DENTISTRY AND MEDICINE**
- **PARENTING**
- **CHILDREN BOOKS**
- **PHILOSOPHY**

In 2003, he founded Mdex, a dental company upon which in 2018, he launched the most ambitious private endeavour to reform the dental industry, Canada wide. Philosopher, he has close to his heart the quest of happiness of the people surrounding him, patients and colleagues alike. In 2020, he launched an International collaborative initiative named **THE ALPHAS** to share knowledge and for Entrepreneurs and Doctors to thrive through the Greatest Pandemic and Economic depression of our time.

In 2016, he co-found with Tranie Vo, Emotive World Incorporated, a tech research company to use technology to empower happiness and sharing. U.A.X. the ultimate audio experience is the landmark project on which the team is advancing, utilizing the technics of the movie industry and the advancement in ARTIFICIAL INTELLIGENCE to save the book industry and to upgrade the continuing education space.

These projects have allowed Dr Nguyen to attract interests from the international and diplomatic community and he is now the center of a global discussion in the wellbeing and the future of the health profession. It is in that matter that he shares his thoughts and encourages the health community to share their own stories.

"It's not worth it go through it alone! Together, we stand, alone, we fall."

Motivational speaker and serial entrepreneur, philosopher and author, from his own words, Dr Nguyen describes himself as a dentist by circumstances, an entrepreneur by nature and a communicator by passion.

He also holds recognitions from the Canadian Parliament and the Canadian Senate.

POWERPLAY
HOW TO BUILD THE PERFECT TEAM

by Dr. BAK NGUYEN

INTRODUCTION
BY Dr. BAK NGUYEN

CONCLUSION
BY Dr. BAK NGUYEN

INTRODUCTION
BY Dr. BAK NGUYEN

This is a surprise for me, to write yet another book at the dawn of 2021. Actually, I am starting my 78th book, **POWERPLAY, HOW TO BUILD THE PERFECT TEAM** on the last day of 2020, December 31.

It is the dawn of the day, everyone is still sleeping. In other words, I have the whole day. But I highly doubt that I will have finished this book before midnight. Or maybe?

In 2 hours, I have an interview to give, launching **THE RISE OF THE UNICORN** co-written with my friend and mentor, Dr. Jean De Serres. Joining us is newly appointed anchor, Brenda Garcia. It is a book launch, an interview, but also the launch and discussion of a new company, the **UNICORN**.

I thought I would have some free time after, but no, another executive meeting is following on the matter of hundreds of millions in investment for another venture. My schedule was full before the idea of writing yet another book.

Since Christmas this year, I already wrote and completed 2 new books, **THE RISE OF THE UNICORN 2** and **THE VACCINE, A TALE OF SPIES AND ALIENS**. Sure, the second one is a book for kids, co-written with William Bak, but still, that's a lot of work. The book is ready, the audiobook too, thanks to the **ECHO PROTOCOL**, only the imaging is left to be negotiated with the artists.

For the **RISE OF THE UNICORN 2**, I got inspired by our last sprint to the finished line as AMAZON, APPLE, and BARNES and NOBLE were approving **THE RISE OF THE UNICORN 1** within hours. Since it was COVID Christmas and that I was stuck home, I decided to travel, differently.

Even my co-author Jean has no idea of the existence of the second volume at the time of the writing of these lines. He will learn about it on air, in about 2 hours! And of course, I will invite him to join in! I've written 8 chapters, nearly 20,000 words, only the conclusion is to be written, after Jean's part. To me, that's a done deal.

Logic would dictate me to take some hours off before the interview and before the end of the year. But I woke up this morning with that feeling that I was still leaving something unfinished: 2020!

To be honest and bold, 2020 has been a shitty year to everyone, literally everyone on the planet. Even if, some rose from the opportunity, the stress and adaptation, the restrictions, the death toll, the anxiety… 2020 is a year that must end in order for a new one, a better one to start, better and with hope.

For the last months, I was reaching out to all the people I meet, to find a symbolic way to flush down 2020 and to start fresh 2021. No one came back to me with a symbolic with viral power. I can't blame them, I did not find one myself… until just now.

I was looking to flush out 2020, how about welcoming 2021 instead? Reality will be that 2020 will be a turning point in the lives of most of us, if not all of us.

For the last year, I've been talking about the **AGE OF COLLABORATION** through my books, interviews, and Alpha summits. Now, the trend is picking up and more and more people are referring to the **AGE OF COLLABORATION**.

And this is how this journey, the last of 2020 came to the table: to draft a clear portrait of the past versus the future. Yes, **POWERPLAY** is about building a team, God knows that if we are to win the COVID war, now, more than ever, we must come together and collaborate.

For the past months, we've been obedient and trusting the authority and our governments. Many mistakes have we endured. Some rebelled, causing even more harm to the collective. I suggested that we rebuild instead. Actually, we have no choice but to rebuild. To rebuild what and how, those are now the questions.

I will talk from my perspective, as an entrepreneur.

"Entrepreneurs are builders. Empower the entrepreneurs and you have a driving force leading with hope and concrete solutions."
Dr. BAK NGUYEN

Entrepreneurs and business people, were heavily challenged this last year. Why are they more important than others? Because they are the driving force that will employ and put to work the rest of the population. Because their work and creations are what giving us a sense of life as we know it.

You are hungry, where do you go. Either to the supermarket or the restaurant: you are visiting entrepreneurs. You are happy and looking to have fun, where do you go? Shopping, skiing, or to spoil yourself with a massage: again, you are within the care of entrepreneurs. You need information and to acquire new skills, especially at this time, where do you turn to? The internet, once again, entrepreneurs.

Entrepreneurs are everywhere and can be everyone. Then, from their vision and initiative, others will join and help them service more and more people. And soon, a company is built, a brand is born.

This is why, to celebrate 2021, I am welcoming you on this journey, one of building the perfect team. One to empower the entrepreneur to lead the way to a better future, to hope, to heal.

I highly doubt that I would finish this book before the new year, but I can assure you that by the time that you have finished your celebrations, and are ready to embrace the new year, the new era, the book will be ready and available on the major outlets, both in printed and audio version.

This is my gift to you: a sprint of inspiration in the spirit of sharing and collaborating for the new ERA at our door: **THE AGE OF COLLABORATION**.

This is **POWERPLAY, HOW TO BUILD THE PERFECT TEAM.**

There are **employees** and **teams.**
There are **unions** and **ambassadors**
There are **liabilities** and assets.
Leverage them well to win.

Dr. BAK NGUYEN

CHAPTER 1
"THE ABSOLUTE QUESTION"
BY Dr. BAK NGUYEN

This journey is about building the perfect team. But since nobody is perfect and that you are not perfect yourself, how do you build something perfect from imperfect components?

"Forget perfection, perfection is a big fat lie!"
Dr. BAK NGUYEN

I don't think that I can be any more straight forward than that! So now that we have put perfection aside, the new element emerging is **COMPONENT**. Yes, even if we are talking about people, from a team standpoint, we are a component of the team. Some components are bigger and of vital importance, some components are smaller, maybe not vital, but as important to keep the integrity of the system.

So a team is really that, a system, and the people, its components. What is holding the team together? Really, do you ever ask yourself that question?

Whatever you are building your first team or managing a staff of 3000 people, the question is the same: what is keeping the team together. At 3000 employees, you might have a long list of answers… those help, but they are not it. If you have a team of 2, is the answer any easier to find?

What is holding the team together, either it is 3000 people or 3 people is the **ABSOLUTE QUESTION**:

"Why are we putting a team together for?"

Once you have a short, clear, and definite answer to that **ABSOLUTE QUESTION**, you have what it takes to build a team that will last. By saying that your team will last, I am not saying that all the members will stay forever, but your team will, your culture will. We will come back to the **CULTURE** question later on.

For now, let's focus on the **WHY** of your team. To make money is not a good answer, because before you can make money with a team, you will have to invest much time, energy, and money to build that team and to see to its maintenance. So to make money is not your answer.

Is it to multiply your impact? Is it to save time? Is it to cover more territories? Is it to strengthen some weaknesses of your existing team? Is it to create a possible ripple effect in your community? To each his or her answer.

The exact reason why you need a team is yours, but know that its exactitude will make or break you. Build a team for the wrong reasons (those that matter to you) and your team will be a burden, much more than an empowerment.

So here comes the core of the question, what is the team to you? It is that relationship that is the **ABSOLUTE QUESTION**. By going through the process, you are introspecting yourself and recognizing what you lack and what you are looking for in others. You might be the best in your field, but recognizing that you have your boundaries is always the first step in the building of a team.

> "Even if you are good, with a team, you can become great!
> If you are already great, with a team, you could last forever!"
> **Dr. BAK NGUYEN**

That's the spirit. If you can see where your team would lead you, if you can feel the power and the impact you will have with the support of a team, now you are ready to start recruiting. And why this moment of narcissism? Because that is the only empowerment you will have for a long while.

You see, building a team is about inspiring, nurturing, and depending on their results to advance. If you think that your team, those people you have recruited, trained, and paid, are there to serve you, well, you are in for a long and bad ride. You are there to empower and to serve them!

Of course, the servitude model will work at first, but always, at every single task, your team will be an expense, a burden, and a liability to you. If all you are looking for is a service in exchange of a fee, you are better hiring consultants and experts, not hiring a team.

The consultants and experts are immediate "*upgrades*" to your forces, they are like mercenaries in an army. They are expensive and will have to be renegotiated after each campaign, after each journey. It might work, but your culture will be one of mercantilism. That was okay if it was aligned with your core intentions. Was it?

And the danger with that model is that for as long as you are right and the money is cash flowing positively, you can keep the system balanced. As soon as the winds change, that money is scarce and that people are leaving, what do you have left? Solely yourself and your culture of paying for service. Now without money or with much less money, you have nothing left to build back with, since your core culture was money and that money is now gone.

In the other situation, with a team, even if the people inside of your team might change through the year, your team still evolves and the spirit of each action, each decision, is leaving an imprint that becomes the culture of your company, its legacy. Even broken, a company has a chance to come back, to reborn from its ashes, like a Phoenix, thanks to its culture.

You want a clear example? Without naming a company, one of today's biggest companies was once facing bankruptcy. Its coming back was based on its reputation and on the reputation of one of its co-founders. People believed, that's what gave the company a second chance to rise even higher than its first breakthrough. Of course, I am talking about a household name.

A team and a culture will not save every enterprise from its demise, but it's one of the aces a leader will need to hope for a chance of success of coming back.

That being said, nobody is building a team just in case of failure or bankruptcy. We are building a team to materialize a vision, to build and to service people, from an idea to a product or service. And that service or product is our way to make the world a little better, a little more efficient, a little happier.

So whatever is your dream, ask yourself that **ABSOLUTE QUESTION** first, what is the reason for your team to be? And once you are feeling one with your answer, then, you are ready to build, recruit, and to manage a team.

At **Mdex & Co**, my company of 17 years, I had many employees and team members throughout the years. Some were partners, some others were guests, most were employees. I grew from a single dental chair clinic into a company with the promise to change the entire industry. On that banks are investing millions, year after year.

I have to tell you that my growth was not done without paying a high price, sometimes, a very high price. When you are a small team, each member is like family to you. That starts the relationship very well, one might think.

Well, it is not. It might buy you a great beginning, but soon enough, the comparison factor will sit in and poison your relations, even worse, your work environment.

Not everyone wants the same thing. What makes sense to you as a visionary and a builder is pure danger and risk to most of your employees. If they are your family, will you submit yourself and your vision to a vote? Even if that sounds noble, what kind of growth you should expect from that path?

What happen in my own company is that my team and family were able to follow the evolution for a while. From one chair into three. From one clinic into two. From being cool into being the prominent player. But when it was time to repackage all of what we learned into a company and a bluechip, I lost almost all of them.

I am not kidding you, except for my co-founder and some core members, they all left in waves, as a protestation. They did not understand the vision and did not support it. For my defense, I did spend tens of thousand on change and transition experts to bridge the gap. But the gap was too great, the ambition was too big.

Since each team member was someone that I recruited, trained, and nurtured myself, they were like family to me. At each departure, I suffered a new blow. I was deeply hurt, every single time.

And I moved on and kept building my vision. I recruited new team members and we built **Mdex** into the UNICORN it promises to be today, in the dental field. One changing the way that dentistry is delivered, one changing the rapport of a dentist to his or her profession, one changing the experience of the patients drastically, one changing the work environment of the staff and team members for the better.

If that is of interest to you, I will invite you to look for **CHANGING THE WORLD FROM A DENTAL CHAIR**, my 7th book, written to defend my nomination as Ernst and Young Entrepreneur of the year. I got the nomination, but did not win the grand prize. But that brought me on the world stage. That story is available on all major platforms. You can even experience it as an **U.A.X.**, an audio-movie experience streaming on Spotify.

And how did I survived the massive departure of my team members? Because we had a culture. You see, my reason to have a team in the first place, was to better serve my patients. When my team left, I was still greeting my patients and making sure that they were leaving happy and satisfied.

Our patients keep coming in. In fact, they even referred more and more of their friends, family, and colleagues. I hired a director of human resources and we were back in business, much more stronger than before, tripling our workforce within months.

I was very hurt by the departures. But once again, I was remembered that my love story was one with my patients. My patients, they are the one who kept the lights on and the wind blowing in our favor. On that, my proof is that the most ambitious private project ever financed by a bank in the dental field, was made possible by someone I met in my dental chair!

Today, I have transferred that same culture to my team, the love story that I share with my patients. They are inspired by it and are now doing a better job than me, empowering and nurturing such quality relationships with our patients.

The Mdex community never ceased to grow. Today, most of the patients making Mdex the success that it is, I never even met with them. My team, whatever its faces, my team, through the face of diversity, of integrity, of professionalism, and above all, with a friendly smile and gentle intentions is ensuring the legacy and the continuity of the company.

> "Know yourself, know the other, and then, only then, you may deal."
> Dr. BAK NGUYEN

CHEAT SHEET

So what I want you to do is very straightforward. Write down on a piece of paper why you have a team. Then, read it out loud. If your answer made sense to you, then, you can move on to the second question.

How much are you paying your team? Is that justified with the answer to your **ABSOLUTE QUESTION**? And again, write down your answer and read it out loud. Only you will be the judge, but take the time to weigh that answer of yours.

If that still makes sense, now we are having fun. Ask yourself how much more would you need in order to double that team of yours?

This is **POWERPLAY, HOW TO BUILD THE PERFECT TEAM.**

There are **employees** and **teams**.
There are **unions** and **ambassadors**
There are **liabilities** and **assets**.
Leverage them well to win.

Dr. BAK NGUYEN

CHAPTER 2
"THE HAMSTER TRAP"
BY Dr. BAK NGUYEN

Now that you have confirmed the reason for the existence of your team, and your commitment to support and to grow that team, let's review what else can go wrong.

Hiring and recruiting are not easy, but anyone with time and some resources can interview people and decide who is the best qualified or the less incompetent to fill a position. On that, here is my position: I rather keep an empty position than to fill it will someone that will tank my entire team!

In other words, to the saying that everyone deserves a shot, I will give that chance to someone with the will to fit in the team and to be a team player. While most people looking for a job are saying that they are eager to start and to learn, you have to look into that person's eyes and try to see through.

What is that person really wants? What motivates that person? Can that person be motivated? Can that person bring something positive to the team?

No team is perfect, that I can tell you. But most teams have a dynamic, a certain harmony, or even a competitive edge challenging one another to keep the team advancing forward. Are you empowering those traits of your team, or, with the newly hired, you are inserting a disruptive element. Mark my words, it was not personal, it was about the team spirit and dynamic.

This is mainly the reason why I do believe that whoever is taking care of the hiring, must have at his or her side a manager from the field, one who knows his teammates on a first name basis. It is not about building the perfect happy family, it is about balancing the forces in play.

If you are alone and are hiring your first employee, ask yourself the same question, how would that person fit into my team of 2? Now, here is what interesting. You are an entrepreneur risking your saving, your career to launch an enterprise. Usually, you are doing so because you know you have a special talent that allows you to be better than the average Joe. That's why you are starting your own company in the first place.

You do not have much money and you are trying to keep the expenses under control since you are spending much and haven't brought in enough, yet. Who are you hiring? An equal? I hope that was true, but the odds are that you will be hiring someone you can afford, not a double of yourself. In that case, on what conditions do you evaluate that person?

How can someone with much fewer qualifications, experience, and most of the time, motivation than you, be in harmony with that team of 2 that you are building? Well, my first advice to you is never to hire only 1 person into your team. You need to balance the forces.

Since you are more "Powerful" you need to hire 2-3 employees, not one. By doing so, you will have a team to balance with. It might take time, patience, and some failures, but the chances that all 3 of your team members all fail at the task of fitting in, are rather slim. Unless your system has a flaw and that no one can fit into your requirement.

Even in that extreme case of failure, you will be facing an upside, since you will have to identify the mistake right away: you! When that happens, you need to come back at the **ABSOLUTE QUESTION** and answer it again and again. That is the best way to keep your pride at bay.

"Leadership has nothing to do with being bossy."
Dr. BAK NGUYEN

Many people think that being a leader is calling the shots and making the decisions. Well, I can tell you that it is merely the first step of a leader in *pilot mode*. As a leader, you are looking to understand the people and the systems. Your job is to keep the system running smoothly and to keep it running, no matter what.

For those building from scratch, you are building a system. You will still need to rely on most of the other systems you are borrowing and renting to keep your doors open. No one is in business to reinvent the wheel.

So resist the temptation to have everything perfect and moving your way. For as long as it is working, let it be. Then, if you still have time and energy to spare, before addressing that flaw, ask yourself if you will be gaining more or losing more addressing that same flaw. Now you understand what it is to be a leader.

A leader knows that to every call that he or she makes, there are consequences and a ripple effect. Make sure that the ripple effect is either a positive one with synergy to your journey or at least, one that won't disturb the balance of your team and systems in place.

So entrepreneurs in a leadership position are not the wisest nor the boldest, but if they successfully evolve from their position, they all grow to become much more reserved and cautious individuals. They will prefer the system to auto-correct itself rather than to impose their views and have to deal with its counter effect, trusting the auto-correction to their team.

So no, being a leader is not ordering people around. Actually, being a leader is the exact opposite of that, it is to inspire people to take a small leadership role and to take their place in the system under your watch.

This is what I've learned throughout the years. This will be true for a new CEO or Vice-President coming into function. What about the founders? Well, the founders are from another breed.

Founders are super entrepreneurs and champions at what they do. They have mastered special skills and have learned so many other skills on the way, not by passion, but out of necessity. They are the students by excellence. They lead by example and they are always there to save the day. They are the champions of their enterprise. They are the champions for their clients. They are the champions of their team. Are they?

They might be the champion of their business and the champion to the clients, but they are not the champion of their team, even if they are the ones signing the check of each employee. I will cut to the chase.

> **"Be a champion and you are running right into the hamster trap, the wheel of fortune!"**
> Dr. BAK NGUYEN

Think of it for a minute. If you are the champion of your enterprise, who is on the mind of everyone to call in case of emergency? You! If you are the champion to each of your clients, who do they want every time that they are at the door? You! You are not running a business, you are the business! And you are always running!

So within the same perspective, how do you think that your employees are looking at you? Like the person to beat. What you think was inspirational, was in fact, the seed to the comparison. It will be you and them. Eventually you versus them!

But you were treating them like family! Even worse! Now they will hate you because of that. At some point, they thought that you were equals or close, how do you think that they will be reacting as you are constantly showing them how small they are beside you? And I am not even addressing the issue of those overprotective and micromanaging.

You never want to establish a culture of you versus them. They are your team, you are the one paying them! You should be one!

So what is the solution to that problem? First, forget about the hero and the champion complex. If you are an entrepreneur and a leader, the first thing in your heart should be *compassion* and *humility*. I said humility, not a lack of confidence. Humility is to not step over someone else and to recognize the value of each person. Confidence is to occupy your space, completely and without doubt nor hesitation.

So once you have reminded yourself why you need a team in the first place, that should put humility and confidence in their rightful place. You are the driver of the business. You have established direction and culture, your team should empower that. Then, it is your job to empower them to be at their best, fitting in the system that you've set.

As you are hiring more than one person each time, you are diluting the comparison opposition of 2. You also need to be the bigger man or woman in the room, every time, since now they are more of them versus one of you! So how do you solve that new situation of them versus you? With a mission and a goal to achieve, the reason why you have hired them in the first place.

"Give your team a challenge and a clear direction, and trust them to make you proud. Then, be there to empower and to help them on their mission."
Dr. BAK NGUYEN

Otherwise, you are building a public that you are paying that will hate you for every victory that you are bringing in. You are the super hamster running in a wheel, feeding those who are waiting for you to fall, and will be whispering: "I knew that he was not perfect!"

CHEAT SHEET

This one is very simple. Ask yourself why are you hiring a team? Write that down on a piece of paper, once more. Read it out loud.

Ask yourself what have you sacrificed to build your enterprise? Please write down each of the sacrifices and the prices that you've paid. Read them out loud.

Then ask yourself, are those worth more than the comfort of the pride to always be the best and the illusion of perfection? Please, write down your answer and read it out loud. Twice if you must. But listen to your answer.

Your team can be what you need them to be. Either people doing what you've started, or a public judging you, eating popcorn and waiting for your demise. It is your choice. Do you still want to be the champion? The hamsters?

This is **POWERPLAY, HOW TO BUILD THE PERFECT TEAM.**

There are **employees** and **teams**.
There are **unions** and **ambassadors**
There are **liabilities** and **assets**.
Leverage them well to win.

Dr. BAK NGUYEN

CHAPTER 3
"WE EACH HAVE A PLACE IN THE SYSTEM"
BY Dr. BAK NGUYEN

Is that the only way to build a team? No. But this is surely the ideal for which you must aim for. Keep in mind that nothing is ever perfect, so free yourself from that burden. You will need all of your resources to face the real problems on the ground.

At Mdex, I struggled with that Hero complex for a long, very long time. I built a company from the ground up with not much resources but my will and my name. Add to that, that I was a misfit as a dentist (I became one to honor my immigrant parents), and you have an idea of the conditions of my humble beginnings.

Then, one by one, I connected with my patients and make a name for myself. I learned the inside and out of the profession, but as a dentist, I also learned the inside and out of management, of human resources, of banking, of accounting, of taxes implications... well, I had to learn everything. I knew much without knowing it all.

Instead of thinking that I was the best of everything, I considered that doing my MBA, Master in Business Administration. My way of seeing it was that I got paid to learn, on the ground.

This is how I swallow the late nights, the extra hours, and all of the mistakes to pay every time someone from my team dropped the ball. Because this is really what it means to be in a leadership position, when someone dropped the ball, you are the one who will need to fix it.

Doing that, I was very much appreciated by those I was serving, my patients. My name and reputation were growing and expanding. From the beginning, I never wanted my name on the company, but the name of a team, a brand. Mdex was the contraction of Medicine and Expertise. That was my first move to building a team.

People joining in (the team members) knew that there was a place for them to perform and to grow. People coming in to hire us (the patients) did not know who they will be meeting. That was a problem. so I had to work twice as hard to build a culture and a promise that patients would love.

"Mdex, for joy for life."
Dr. BAK NGUYEN

That tagline made people laugh at us at the beginning. We were dentists talking about joy and life. But slowly, my warmth and humanity got transposed to my team and a culture of joy and happiness emerged from the sweat on the ground.

At that point, everyone willing to learn, and having joy at their core could evolve with us. They still needed to meet with the legal and licensing boards. It was a very soft integration. To support the culture of joy, I let each and every one of my team members to find their place. I even told them:

> **"If I have to be your boss, it is the beginning of the end of our relationship."**
> **Dr. BAK NGUYEN**

I pushed the ball as far as I could with my co-founder seconding each of my decision. On that, Tranie Vo, my wife, best friend, and partner was my rock, through thick and thin. We learned on the field together, we grew together into a dynamic duo.

If I was managing, she was taking care of marketing and expanding our market shares. If I was in operation, she was managing and leading the support staff. If I was building an expansion, she was aligning the finances and keeping things flowing smoothly. Today she is the COO, Chief operating officer of the company.

Well, even between us, we needed time to adjust and to learn to respect one another while putting our best on the table. Actually, it took us close to 15 years before becoming a power couple recognized by the industry. The key here is always to come back to the core: "Why do I need a team?"

Even at our beginning, as a team of 2, we always kept that question at our core, every time we were discouraged, in a fight, about to give up on each other, that was the glue holding us back from doing something we would regret later on.

It took much sweat to build but that relationship proves to be the rock on which we built our company. That rock gave me the confidence I needed to go out there and to perform as a dentist that people would love. That confidence allows us to recruit, manage, and have people to join our vibe, at least for a given time. Because we were a team.

"Nothing will last forever. The sooner you accept that concept, the stronger and wiser you will be."
Dr. BAK NGUYEN

We built a system, one with culture, one with philosophy, one with a history and a legacy. In our team, I am the sensitive one, one attached to people, and our history. Well, that warmth made the success of Mdex. That warmth also brought it to almost meet its end, as I was trying to convince people looking for stability to evolve and to embrace the future.

What I really learned from the experience is to not hold back anyone from evolving, including myself. As we are blessed with a great moment together, I enjoy every minute of that moment. As that moment come to pass, I will keep the best souvenirs in my heart and let go of the rest.

If it is given that our paths cross again, I will welcome that encounter as I embrace every new encounter. This is what saved Mdex and allowed me to build a company supported by the people and the finance industry.

So in the case of Mdex, my team has three components. The patients, the staff, and the management. The balance and prosperity arrive as one successfully align these three components. That is the old model of every enterprise. In the new model of Mdex, I am breaking down the staff component into partnership components, so people will be working for themselves, with ownership and pride.

We are still establishing the new philosophy at Mdex, but slowly, our team is adapting and adopting. And why are we doing so? Because there is no better motivated employee than one working for him or herself! Having said that, am I getting further from my **ABSOLUTE QUESTION**?

Mine was to have a team to better serve the patients. Elevating my staff into partners, I am ensuring that they will be at their best to serve their patients!

My ways and their expressions may have changed throughout the years, but my core and promise to my patients still remain the same: FOR JOY FOR LIFE!

Today, I am not the hero nor the champion of my company anymore. I am an inspirational leader, one attracting investors to invest in our vision. My team of HR is taking care of the recruitment, of hiring and training. I am at their service to give them an appealing recruitment call. I am also at their service to keep the employees motivated and happy.

I am still seeing my patients, and on that, I keep delivering the highest and smoothest standard of care. That is a promise between me and my patients. But the culture of the company has grown and taken its place. I must tell you today that most of my patients consider my staff as much as they are considering me.

To me, as a leader, it is the uttermost sign of success, that my vision and culture have transcended me. And every time, it is a celebration for us. I am strong and loved.

My team is looking up to me and is asked to reach the same result, helping people. Well, every time that they are in a difficult position, they are trying harder to impress me. I thank them for that. Every time that they have a victory, I am the first one celebrating with them. I celebrate their victory because, at a much higher level, they are my best victories.

In order for that to arrive, you need to trust your team and to provide them with the tools and the space to execute. Everyone will have their own unique way. They still have to operate within the boundaries of the company, but the more they feel that they can personalize it, the more efficient and involved they are at their task.

At Mdex, that meant to shift the vision of being a patient of the clinic to become your patient. On the matter, we do give our staff certain latitude to find a way to better serve their patients. A certain degree of flexibility within the organization has empowered our staff to take a leadership role and to improve our process and politics.

So if I have to summarize this chapter into one paragraph, keep your **ABSOLUTE QUESTION** very close to your heart. Then, try to stop being the boss and the champion as soon as possible, to become a mentor, inspiring people to score and to impress you.

Then, give them the means and power to be better than you! They will love you for it. Prepare to be impressed!

CHEAT SHEET

Remember that as an entrepreneur in a leadership position, your role is to support a system, not individuals, especially, not yourself. To build a system, you need to be confident enough to let go and to trust others to build better than you could do it yourself. Actually, to be a leader, you will need to believe in that, at your core.

Of course, they won't be beating you at your own game on the first day. Give them some time, believe in them, empower them, and soon enough, you will be surprised with how close they are catching up to you. Soon, they will be teaching you!

This is no joke. Today, for most of the administrative tasks in my company, my team all know better to not ask me since I have no idea of the answer. Often, it is me that go to them for help and answers.

I am still the champion in my field as I am an operator, a surgeon, but that's it! And even on that, I am actively teaching to new recruits my skills and craft so they can eventually replace me, even to be better than me.

And the day that my proteges will be better than me, that day I will be most successful, because that day, I am leading a company, not a personal career.

Know what you want and open up. Recruit, train, and trust. Then be confident enough to let go and to observe. If you want a team that you will consider perfect eventually, that is how the story will be built. We each have to take our place in the system.

And if you have empowered each of them to grow and to reach their full potential, you might have a chance to stay in their memory as the best opportunity they ever had.

This is **POWERPLAY, HOW TO BUILD THE PERFECT TEAM.**

There are **employees** and **teams**.
There are **unions** and **ambassadors**
There are **liabilities** and **assets**.
Leverage them well to win.

Dr. BAK NGUYEN

CHAPTER 4
"SCARCITY"
BY Dr. BAK NGUYEN

Now we know how to build and to keep a team motivated. Practically, where do you recruit good people? Especially in this age in which in North America and Europe, we are falling victims to the reverse demographic pyramid, having more people leaving the workforce than younger people coming in.

As the workforce is narrowing down and as competition and productivity are asking more and more specificity and expertise, how do you cope, HR wise?

The biggest companies have turned to technology to cope with the lack of available workforce. In supermarkets, to scan your own purchase and to self-service is becoming, more and more, a new norm. The entrepreneurs are implementing those, not to save, but to cope with the scarcity of employees. The public is empowering the trend because it is faster, not cheaper, faster.

And that trend is one on the rise. Your purchases on the web are handled by more A.I. and systems, humans are now only a component of the system, not the whole system as there were a few years earlier. So this is a major shift.

That major shift has put more pressure on the recruitment process since the jobs are now often much more task-specific and knowledge-heavy. Knowing that the pool of the available workforce is narrowing down, how do you compete to recruit the best people to join your team?

I won't lie to you, in some cases, HR is just thrilled to have interviews scheduled. They are telling me that it feels more like the potential employee is interviewing them, not the other way around! Well, this is a new reality, you will have to adapt to it.

My advice is to keep your standards and philosophy. Above all, resist the temptation to lower your standard just to save the day, you will be causing much more harm than good in the long run.

This is true rather you a starting a new team or recruiting to reinforce your existing team. To get someone in the door that does not fit your culture and that has no chance nor motivation to ever meet them, well, you are pulling the whole team back.

"But that's ok, it is just me. I am strong, that person won't drag me down." Those are the kind of lies that new entrepreneurs will feed themselves with. Well, remember that an enterprise is a relationship between the customers and the service and experience. If you are tanking the experience or even worse, the service, you are losing customers and tanking your reputation. All of that because one could not smile?!

If that person is in the back office, without contact with any customers, but still has that lack of ability to meet with your culture, you will never trust that person. So you just hired a new responsibility for yourself, to double-check on the delegated tasks.

That, by itself, is bad. Worst, is the tracks of habits that you are developing, micromanaging, and not trusting your team. Remember, a company is a system, it is about the team, not the individual. But you, as the founder, for now, are still the core of the team. Your philosophy and habits are the culture of your enterprise. Will you have a culture of mistrust and micromanagement?

If you have a bigger team, the effects will take more time to arrive to your ears, but what I just described as a scenario, well it is your team that will absorb the shock and its ripple effects. Trust me, soon enough you will have to deal with the consequences!

So give people a chance to fit in, but choose those with the will and potential to fit in. This is why in the previous chapters I asked you to look your potential staff in the eyes and ask yourself what motivates them? Can they be motivated? And then, are you equipped to provide such empowerment?

"Do not tolerate or average down. Inspire, and empower."
Dr. BAK NGUYEN

Very well then, but about the scarcity of the workforce? How do you address it? The first and logical thing to do is to recruit where everyone is recruiting, posting on the boards, and having posts or head hunters helping. This is fishing. Still, you must do it. Just do not count solely on its results if you are hoping for success.

If you have taken the time to build a team that is embodying the culture of your enterprise, look to them for recruitment. Usually, people are gathering in similar crowds, mentality, and social standing. Offer your staff an incentive to referer friends and family. Give them the recognition when you hire someone they have referred. You just found a new streamline of recruitment. To them, you have offered them influence.

Do you know that more than remuneration, influence, and recognition are on the top of your team wish list? The referral solution can never be your only stream of hiring, but it is a great alternative plan. So we are back at the fishing pool.

Well, you try to attract alikes. How about looking in the other direction? Diversity is your answer! I know, the term diversity is a trendy one, to be open and to welcome the immigrants and blablabla.

Let's take a moment a look passed the color of the skin and the accent of these people. We are not hiring people to look good, we are looking to fill our ranks and positions. They have values and are highly motivated to gain back what they lost, leaving their country. They have skills and expertise. Be open to give them a chance, keeping your standards as is.

Some will fit and some won't. The odds were the same as with the other candidates. But once you have successfully integrated a member from diversity into your team, you now have access to his or her power of attraction too. If you treat them as ambassadors to your brand, like you are doing with your other employees, chances are that they can open new networks of clients and of hiring to you. Those networks you may not have access to before.

So your solution scarcity is to embrace diversity, once you have a solid culture and enough respect for your employees to elevate them to the status of ambassadors of your company.

"In a leadership position, you are empowering, not ordering."
Dr. BAK NGUYEN

So if you multiply the networks through diversity, you now have more and more streams of hiring, of revenue. Scarcity, at a larger scale, might be the same, but you are doing much better than your competition, at least in terms of hiring.

At the beginning of this chapter, I mentioned that my HR people were telling me that the position seems reversed nowadays, that they feel like it is the future employees who are interviewing the company. Well, with referees, you do not have that problem. They are coming to you. Be gracious and offer them a better deal than they could have hope for, and you have kickstarted a hiring with better odds.

That referral now is accountable, not only to you but to the person who have referred him or her. Your employees referring, will take pride in making sure they have contributed to the future of the company. Doing so, that success will empower more team members to do the same. And now, you just have another system in place, one helping you to defeat scarcity.

"Making your team your best success.
Then, elevate them into your ambassadors"
Dr. BAK NGUYEN

CHEAT SHEET

Look at your workforce and name everyone. Write down their names. Then, ask yourself who would you love to have a double of. Go to that person, make him or her the exact compliment, of how much you would wish to hire a twin of them. And ask for their help.

65

There is no downside to this since you are empowering your team. If they have someone to refer they will, but now, you just gain an ambassador, one making sure that your culture and value will prevail! It is not about you anymore, it is now about him or her too!

Repeat the exercise with all the team members that you wish you would have a twin of. Do that privately. Give it some time, and as the first success comes in, make the thank you public and use that opportunity to invite the rest of your team to join in the ambassador program.

Doing so, you will be doubling on empowerment. Whatever the result, your team will get stronger and stronger. You just have established a new culture.

Then, I want you to have a talk with your HR department and them to open up to diversity without lowering the company culture standard. Like anything, it will take time, but you now have opened up your company to a new network.

This is **POWERPLAY, HOW TO BUILD THE PERFECT TEAM.**

There are **employees** and teams.
There are **unions** and ambassadors
There are **liabilities** and assets.
Leverage them well to win.

Dr. BAK NGUYEN

CHAPTER 5
"CROSS-PLATFORMING"
BY Dr. BAK NGUYEN

In the last chapter, we discussed the great potential of having your employees to become ambassadors of your brand and leveraging the status of diversity of your team to open new networks. I would like to come back on that.

Everything that I mentioned in the last chapter is true and working. Only, we need to precise the diversity employee opening up new networks of business. This does not happen often. And, for it to happen, that employee of yours should share the same social status as the clients that you are trying to seduce. This is the only way it will be successful.

Each business is servicing a very targeted and specific clientele. Try, when possible, to recruit employees and team members from that same crowd. Those consuming your products and services are the best ambassadors of your brand.

The cars and dealership industries have long understood that rule, lending a demo car to each of their representatives. The only way one can sell with credibility a product or a service is as he or she has consumed it him or herself. This is not an absolute rule, but one not to be neglected.

I told you about your company culture. Part of that culture is your company's social status and mindset. Different social classes have different mindsets. It is not always possible, but when it is, try to hire the people close to the public they aim to service.

Now, have someone from a higher social class to serve a lower one, if that team member is okay with that, you just found yourself a *Unicorn*. This is how they called it in the HR industry. Well, most of the time, the *Unicorn*, as rare as they are, will be found in the pool of Diversity!

You want an example of the *Unicorn theory*, look at physicians. Not all of them service the people of their social status. But as they service the lower status, they are showing humility. People love that, they love humility and confidence all in one when it comes to who is servicing them. This is will work well within a certain elasticity. But you can't stretch the elastic too much. I believe that with more than 3 layers of social status, the edge is lost and the difference now will be a liability rather than an edge.

It is hard enough to find good employees, left alone looking for *Unicorns*. I am simply saying that when you find one, appreciate him or her and empower them to their best. That being said, this is not the same than to hire an overqualified person.

I've been on the hiring side for most of my life. I can tell you that I was once confusing the overqualified with the unicorn. On paper, they are the same but look into their eyes, and you will see how different those two are.

The *Unicorn* is someone eager to serve, to service. He or she is willing, not overqualified. He or she may be from a higher social class, but servicing was more important to them. What motivated them is the result of their work, not their status. These people, when you find them, never let them go. They are not perfect, they have their edge, but give them what they need and they will over-deliver every single time.

It is not the same with an overqualified person. That person knows that he or she is worth more, but, from the circumstances, is resigned to accept a bargain for less than what he or she is. There is a lot of bitterness in the eyes of that person. Well, until that person has made peace with their own journey and choices, that person is broken and you should stay far away.

As the son of an immigrant myself, I always had much sympathy for these people losing everything and starting fresh in a new country. I respect their effort and I feel their pain. That being said, are they available and ready to embrace their new life, or are they still in denial of their new reality?

Throughout the years, I gave to many overqualified people a chance to fit into my team. On paper, they had everything required. In person, we were peers, we had respect for each other. But every single time, as they were still in denial of their own reality, they were not available to fit in our culture and the opportunity that we were offering them. Bitterness, this is what came out, every single time.

Very stubborn myself, I tried again and again, but always with the same result. The only difference is how long before the bitterness contaminates everything.

"Bitterness kills hope."
Dr. BAK NGUYEN

Never forget that. The title of this chapter is **CROSS-PLATFORMING**. So let address that, to cross-platform. As I told you that some employees might open new networks and businesses, do not count too much on the business they will be bringing in. Stay humble, but do not hope on a prayer!

How about reversing that logic. How about recruiting from your pool of clients? That should be great, no? These people know your products and services inside and out, they are paying for it. These people understand your culture and may already be ambassadors. Why not recruit them and their *twins*?

That was my view for a while too. On paper, that sounds perfect, but reality will prove to be a completely different story. I told you that commerce is a special bond between a business and its customers. In that relationship, the customer is the boss. Well, once that is established, it is very hard to change.

As a customer, they like you and your enterprise because you are doing for them something they cannot do themselves. Cannot, will not, don't know how. So how is it when you are turning the table? The reconversion is hard and too often unfruitful for more than one reason.

They are not willing to lose the dynamic that they already have with you and your business. That is the unwillingness to change and to adapt. The culture they know from your company was from the receiving end only. If they are not open to adapt, they will always act like a customer. And a customer may become a great ambassador, a customer has never been part of the team making things happen.

Some other time, pride will standing in the way. In business, any business and organization, there is a hierarchy, as minimalist as it may be. As a customer, they were near the top of the hierarchy, at least that was they feeling and understanding. To understand the dynamic here, let's refer to Albert Einstein.

"Once a body reaches a higher level of energy,
it will never go back to its original level."
ALBERT EINSTEIN

In other words, by becoming an employee, they are retrograding their status from your original dynamic. And those will rarely end with a great success story to share. It is a little like trying to have a romantic relationship with your best friend, the odds of failure are overwhelming the excitements and sparks. That kills the vibe at its core.

So cross-platforming is not a great idea when it comes to HR and team building. What I will encourage you to do is to leverage the different components to boost your appeal and to attract more and better people.

Make your team happy and talking about how great and happy they feel working at your company. They will attract more customers and employees.

Empower your clients to open up about their experience and satisfaction with you. They too will attract more customers and applicants for your vacant positions.

To cross-platform is great leverage. Just know the rules, how to leverage, and what is working and what is not.

CHEAT SHEET

What I will ask you to do here is to come back at the beginning of this chapter and to read it again. Only this time, take notes. Then, review your notes and try to picture different situations that relate to this, from your own journey. As you are feeling it, only then, can you understand the logic, power, and dangers of **CROSS-PLATFORMING**.

My biggest recommendation is not to learn from trials and error on this one since cross-platforming means to mix the different components of your system, staff, and customers. Well, if you fail, the odds point in that direction, you are losing 2 ends of your system with one mistake. That's not leveraging, that's plain stupid!

Stay away from cross-platforming if you do not understand this chapter nor you can relate to it. There are other ways of recruiting, less risky, and with better odds. Actually, I believe that you might have better odds of finding a *Unicorn* than to succeed, **CROSS-PLATFORMING**.

This is **POWERPLAY, HOW TO BUILD THE PERFECT TEAM.**

There are **employees** and **teams**.
There are **unions** and **ambassadors**
There are **liabilities** and **assets**.
Leverage them well to win.

Dr. BAK NGUYEN

CHAPTER 6
"MOTIVATION"
BY Dr. BAK NGUYEN

Here we are, at the core of our journey. Recruiting is surely a big component of building the perfect team. But let's address the elephant in the room, shall we? How do we keep our team members motivated?

This is the million-dollar question. You might have as many answers as there are experts on the field. Personally, I met with many of them and they all have their special recipe. In here is not my recipe, but my experience.

I dedicated more than half of this journey telling you about the **ABSOLUTE QUESTION** and of culture. There is a reason for that, Only when you have resolved both the absolute question and the question of culture, you might have a way to find a sustainable way to keep the motivation of your team.

I tried them all! Raising the salary, as great as it might sound, people are happy for about 2 weeks. As their first check comes in. By the second one, it is now part of their new normal. I tried with bonuses, well, once again, it is great the first and second time, but by the third, it has lost its novelty effect, and now sounds more like quotas to meet than a bonus to keep people engaged and happy.

I tried job security, giving them all the insurance that they are vital parts of a team. That led to entitlement and the refusal to evolve. I tried job benefits like health insurance including dental. That was a great effect for 2 months, and then, became part of the package coming with the job. More than paying for each of these ways to keep my team happy, it cost me the time and expenses of the HR team, putting things together.

I won't tell you that those are not good ways to motivate your staff. I will tell you that all of these are of short term celebrations. The only thing that keeps your staff motivated and engaged is when they are feeling empowered and feeling part of something greater than themselves.

Have a mission, like going to the moon, NASA like. Have a goal to help 10,000 people. Aim for something that will lift the world and their spirit with it. Then, give them the opportunity and the tools to make a difference in that sense, and you will have empowered your team.

You can only do so as you have recruited the people motivated and sharing a culture of advancement. Then, trust them enough to give them the latitude and flexibility to implement the necessary steps inside of the company to build, ladder by ladder, the stairway to the moon.

One of my dearest friend and mentor, André Châtelain, coaching my HR department told me once:

"If you are a leader, the mistake is always yours. The victory is theirs."
ANDRÉ CHÂTELAIN

This was one of the wisest things I learned that year, HR wise. For your information, André is the former senior first Vice-President of one of our biggest financial institutions here, in Quebec. He is a member of my board of directors and is coaching my HR department as a favor.

As former number 2 of his institution, he was employing thousands of employees and had more than 100 billion in transactions. At that level, you do not try. You make it happen!

"Make it happen."
Dr. BAK NGUYEN

So I found my harmony with my team differently. Over time, I've learned to keep a safe distance from them, but when I am around, I am all there for them. They come to me for guidance, but most of the time, they come to me to announce their victory.

By stop being the champion and the boss, I entrusted them with the power to make it work. Today, they are celebrating their success, looking to impress me.

Lately, we had a financial crisis, facing the COVID war. Well, I told them the truth and ask for their help to face the impossible. And we made it, very smoothly and within the time constraint. If I am still standing as an enterprise after the ravage of the COVID war, it is thanks to my team.

For my part, I keep the excellence in my culture, taking care of my patients. Those working close to me are bathing in the same vibe. Then, they are looking to recreate that vibe with other patients, with other operators.

I told you, today, the success of Mdex, as we are leading the dental industry toward the future, is that I do not know most of the clientele that we are servicing. And yet, they know me, they are referring, they love the promise and the vision.

That is my job, today as a leader. I have to establish and to walk the vision so my team has a direction to aim for. Between the honors, the world records, and the fame, my team will tell you, Dr. Bak is never stopping.

Even if I am lazy and will not hide from that, everyone will tell you that I am leading the charge about working hard and looking for solutions, even when all seems lost.

I have transcended my champion status into a momentum that keeps then inspired. I would love to say understand, but I will settle for inspiration. What I have carefully managed, is to cut the comparison factor out of the equation. I lead the way in impossible tasks they do not even comprehend. That's cool, they look at the attitude and get their inspiration from that.

I inspire my staff and patients, those I meet and touch. Well, my staff is in the ripple effect of that synergy and they are taking over, to grow and to perpetuate the ripple effect. I have to tell you that today, they are doing a much better job than I could have. I only have the merit of being the catalyst.

That's the inspiration. Inspiration works when the right culture is in place. But that won't be enough to safeguard you from the waves, up and downs, and the emotions of human dramas. We are all humans after all.

Well, I had my suspicions, but COVID shed the light on everything, all at once. To keep the harmony of your team, keep things running smoothly. Keep them engaged and empower them. But above all, keep them busy.

For as long as your team is set on a mission, they will come through and deliver. Stop everything abruptly and observe, what happens. The whole system will crumble down in pieces.

> "A team is dynamic, engage them in your vision, empower them to make the difference, and keep them busy."
> Dr. BAK NGUYEN

All HR managers will confirm how stormy were the COVID waves to them. They have to resolve impossible situations, bridged emotional gaps, and face questions they have never been asked before! Why, because our teams lost their focus. Keeping them home and insecure about their future change the dynamic of the team, even the culture of the enterprise is under siege.

And what do you do under such conditions? Well, as a leader, you have to double your own pace to find resources and means to bridge the gaps, before they are of concern to your team. You are the support of your team, remember?

You are their beacon of hope and the bearer of light through the storm. Keep your calm and keep moving forward. Some of your team members will jump ship, some will leave. Do not try to stop them. Wish them luck and keep your focus, the rest of your team is looking at you.

We were talking of champions before. Well, in time of crisis is the time to be that champion that your team and clients will be looking for. Calm and steadiness will be the qualities you are looking for.

And what they see, they feel. If you have a way to make them feel safe. Or at least safer, they will retake their place in the system and keep moving forward, in the right direction. You need to lead the way, they will do the rest.

To summarize the motivation chapter, be constant and loyal to your promise to them. Mine was to empower them so they can better serve our patients. Then, we celebrated their victories. This is empowerment and purpose.

My job is to keep the flow of patients coming in so my staff could stay focus and on mission. To keep them busy is the key. Well had the luxury of a great real-life simulation with COVID. It is not hypothetical anymore, stop the flow for too long and you will break the systems beyond repair.

"Inspire your team, empower them, and trust them to surprise you.
That's how you will keep them engaged
and motivated."
Dr. BAK NGUYEN

This is **POWERPLAY, HOW TO BUILD THE PERFECT TEAM.**

There are **employees** and **teams**.
There are **unions** and **ambassadors**
There are **liabilities** and **assets**.
Leverage them well to win.

Dr. BAK NGUYEN

CHAPTER 7
"POWERPLAY"
BY Dr. BAK NGUYEN

We are about to finish this journey, already? We were just warming up! We've been through the why and how to build and to keep a team, any team. How about building a power team?

The title of this book is **POWERPLAY**, not power team. There was a reason for that. To have an all starts team, you must have a mission that justifies as much power. You must have the resources and the matrix to support such a team. Usually, this will happen in extreme circumstances as leaders and drivers around the world are suddenly expulsed from their environment, facing a global threat.

That treat will have reason of the ego of each superstar player and they will accept to team up to win. And don't be mistaken, if a **POWERPLAY** is formed, it is to win, not to play or to survive. There is not much room to maneuver here since each superstar usually has their own team.

A war, a revolution, or closer to us, COVID would be the kind of events that would allow the emergence of such **POWERPLAY**. We all dream to be part of one, of a **POWERPLAY**. But before that could happen, we must master our skills and leadership first. The laws of physic surrounding a **POWERPLAY** are basically very similar to the one of building a strong duo or trio to start a business.

In a strong duo or trio of co-founder, the first rule is to complete each others. In other words, people with the same skillset and mindsets, those gathering together are a bad fit to become partners since they have the same strengths and the same flaws. In that case, the collaboration did not benefit any of them, just to double their flaws.

Once more, *diversity* would be the key to form a strong duo or trio of co-founders. Diversity of sex, diversity of age, diversity of expertise, diversity of skillset, and diversity of mindset.

What they need to have in common is a strong desire to reach the same goal. That, and enough humility to listen in a given opportunity. Some other time, it will require much confidence to take the lead, amongst equals.

"Equal and diverse."
Dr. BAK NGUYEN

So to all of you looking to build your company, partner up with someone as different compare to you as possible. The more diverse, the stronger you are, as a team. That being said, you will need much confidence to swallow your pride and to build with respect from the difference of your team.

"Build from the differences."
Dr. JEAN DE SERRES

This is the wisdom that I got from my friend and mentor, Dr. Jean De Serres, former CEO of Hema-Quebec, the equivalent of the Red Cross. To build from the difference with respect, that is how a strong team can be built.

Two strong hearts and heads, once in synergy, are very powerful. Three? Much harder to achieve synergy, but once achieved, even stronger. The key is to tune the egos and prides to trust each other with our weaknesses.

"That's the hardest part, to trust someone else with our weaknesses."
Dr. BAK NGUYEN

But once you have established such trust, you have a powerful team. So to review, the laws of physic of building power duos or trios are:

- **to build from diversity**
- **to build with respect**
- **to have a common goal**
- **to have integrity**

Integrity. We did not address that last one. Integrity is to be able to walk our talk. To be what we advertised that we are. Without integrity, there is no trust. And without trust, there is simply no team.

Remember, that for a powerful duo or trio to form, one is entrusting his or her weaknesses to the others. There is not a single chance for success without trust or integrity.

And everyone will say that they have integrity. Only proofs and facts will tell you what to believe. Look in the eyes of that person and gauge his or her soul to feel the truth.

If you are building your team, (in the power duo or trio) the partners you can have are about of your caliber. If you are teaming up with someone of a much higher, unless you have tremendous potential and power to put on the table, that person is your mentor, not your partner.

My best advice is not to seek mentors. They will spot you as you are scoring on the field. Let them come to you. As for your partners, build with someone you trust and someone accessible. Someone with a different skill set than yours.

That's what I did, betting everything I was and had when I started building with Tranie Vo, my girlfriend at that time, today, my wife, business partner, and best friend. We were so different, only love kept us together.

That difference could have kill both our couple and company, but we've prevailed. It took us 5-7 years to find a balance of forces. By year 15, we became a power couple that business people are drawn to.

Respect and diversity were primarily the core of our power. For those of you who are intrigued with that story, I will invite you to read my 8th book, **THE POWER BEHIND THE ALPHA**, co-written with Tranie Vo.

We each have our story. We each have or had partners. That's how we learn and evolve. That was the beginning of our journey as entrepreneurs and our first steps in the journey of leadership.

With maturity and experience, we all learn, sooner or later, to refine our views, to polish our edge, and to dim down our ego. In some rare cases, the original founders will stick and rise together. In most cases, it was temporary. And that's okay. Be grateful and enjoy the moment.

Whatever the journey, it will shape you, nurture your leadership skill, and mature your perspective. As you are becoming a good leader, an alpha player, you might have the chance to join a **POWERPLAY**.

As I said before, a **POWERPLAY** is formed as alpha players are mobilized from a common enemy, someone or something bigger than themselves. And to be part of such **POWERPLAY**, you need these required conditions:

- **Have a great common enemy**
- **Be an alpha player yourself**
- **Have access to other alpha players**

- And to have enough leadership, humility, and diplomacy to build the matrix of collaboration. Amongst alpha players, that will be your main challenge.

The **matrix of collaboration** would be the hardest to form. I can tell you that there is no definitive recipe for that one. You must weigh and counterweigh the personality of each of the members of the team. No one will take an order from someone else, until each will trust the other enough to, once again, entrust their weaknesses to their partners.

Only then, the **POWERPLAY** will be effective, and the comparison will fade to leave the place for genuine connection and collaboration. If you reach such a stage, you have a **POWERPLAY** until the achievement of your goal.

Unfortunately, the team will disband at the completion of the goal, the intention was not to evolve together for the rest of time, but to achieve a specific goal: to win.

On that matter, I have 2 stories to share with you. The first one is the constitution of my board of directors at **Mdex & Co**. I have successfully managed to attract three super veteran superstar entrepreneurs and managers to my table.

They have created billions in values, have managed hundreds of billions, and have led teams of thousands of employees. I successfully attract them thanks to my ambition, my respect, and my honesty.

"Leadership attracts leadership."
CHRISTIAN TRUDEAU

They are all my mentors. Yet, I am the one holding the power, they consider themselves as advisors. How can I build with so much influence and power in my presence, without stepping on any ego? *Balancing*. That's the only way. I continuously have to balance the forces in place and in play.

Most of the time I even have to provoke that balance, becoming the source of disruption to align all my mentors on the same side, to keep me from falling off the cliff. I must tell you that we all respect each other. Respect, ambition and fun, those are what's keeping my mentors onboard.

My job is to impress my mentors and to push their reflections. Their role is to make sure that our path is sustainable and expandable. I must admit that I am not alone balancing the power and influence of that table, Tranie is the gentle hand that will smooth the edges and keeps the smile on every face. That's **Mdex & Co**.

In the midst of the COVID war, at the first confinement, everything stood still for a few weeks. This is when I went international and hosted summits to try to organize the *resistance* and to prepare for what was to come. Well, within a few weeks, I received leaders, overachievers, and movers and shakers from diverse fields, different countries, different continents, all looking to pitch in to help. We formed the **ALPHAS**.

The international organization is really composed of alphas individuals coming together. Well, I made it happened from openness and compassion. Then, I structure the support tools, but only with one specific intention, to empower each individual. That allowed my leadership to rise and to be accepted by the Alphas.

Today, I am the host and the anchor of the Alphas, not a leader, just a catalyst. Together, we influenced, more than once, policy around the world, and we are now planning for what is coming next. Not playing against the actual power, but preparing the field ahead.

We are no secret organization, we are no governments, we are Alphas coming together to help the world to come back from the COVID war. Unfortunately, I am not free to disclose what is coming next on many fronts, but here what I can share: **COVIDCONOMICS**, a world movement to map the future of our life from the trend emerging with the COVID crisis is one of our interest.

I am bringing the **ALPHAS** in here just to share with you that a **POWERPLAY** is possible well you have all the ingredients. You must be ready to take your role and to walk your talk. I invite all of you to follow our work and impact as they unfold.

CHEAT SHEET

You can't build a **POWERPLAY** on your own. You can only prepare for one. Start with a power Duo or Trio and learn to master the balance of the forces. Learn to let go of your ego and to empower your partners.

Then, you will have to learn to accept your flaws. Even harden, you will have to entrust them to your partners. By doing so, you are experiencing synergy.

"Discover, experience, and master synergy
are the thrills of leadership."
Dr. BAK NGUYEN

This is **POWERPLAY, HOW TO BUILD THE PERFECT TEAM.**

There are **employees** and **teams.**
There are **unions** and **ambassadors**
There are **liabilities** and **assets.**
Leverage them well to win.

Dr. BAK NGUYEN

CHAPTER 8
"BALANCING THE SYSTEMS"
BY Dr. BAK NGUYEN

The keyword in the building of a team is **system**. The keyword to perfect in managing your team is **balance**. The keywords in recruitment of your team are **Diversity** and **Ambassador**. And the keyword to the longevity of your team is **empowerment**.

> "Empower diversity into ambassador and balance the systems, this is the secret of building a perfect team."
> Dr. BAK NGUYEN

But who needs a team and for what reason? Skip the **ABSOLUTE QUESTION** and no recipe will ever transform your team from your biggest burden into your biggest asset. It all started with you. Never forget that.

In chapter 7, we went all the way up to the apogee of a team, to the **POWERPLAY**. I could have finished this journey on that high note. But, you know me, I love to respect the dragon numbers, and to finish with... oh, one last thing, Steve Jobs' style.

So what is my one last thing? How about *cheating*? I told you that to build a team, you need a *culture*. For that, you will need to nurture your team, in-house. I also told you that hiring outside experts will not help you since you will only end up with a culture of money for service.

On the progress of my journeys, I realized that nothing is ever absolute. This is how I grew my magnetism and leadership, by leading to yield flexibility, **balancing the forces**. I am always dancing, sometimes leading, sometimes empowering the other to make his or her move.

Just like experienced managers will let their system to auto-correct, I have learned to never look for perfection, nor for the absolute.

"I am looking for harmony and synergy."
Dr. BAK NGUYEN

Bringing this back to HR and the subject of building the perfect team, is there a way to cheat? Yes! And here it is. First, we all start with little or no experience. You do not want to pay for that experience with time since that will be the most expensive way to learn.

Instead, buy that experience, buy that expertise. And please, do not look for a bargain as you are looking to buy expertise.

"If you buy cheap expertise it is not a glass half full that you are buying, it is often the wrong glass to drink from."
Dr. BAK NGUYEN

Trust me on that, I have paid dearly every time that I was looking to save on expertise fees. I always ended up paying much more. So to hire expert consultants are a good way to kickstart your journey as an entrepreneur. I am not looking for a bargain when looking at buying expertise, but I do not have neither the means nor the desire to buy that expertise for too long.

So I hire the expert and give them the mandate to form my team. That's their mandate. What I am paying in dollars, I am saving in time and, more importantly, in costly mistakes.

This is the first cheat. I buy the expertise from the outside to train my team. Then, as my team is growing and gaining its own expertise, I keep the outside consultants on retainer as a second team, as advisors.

This way I am balancing the forces, the outside and the inner forces. Keeping that equilibrium has proved to be one of the wisest moves I could have made as a manager.

Whatever happens, I always have a backup. I have two systems, and I balance them. In business, we are always aiming to win, no matter what, so I could not put all of my hopes and resources solely in one basket.

"Balancing the forces has proven to be my best moves as a leader."
Dr. BAK NGUYEN

Balancing the systems has also another huge advantage, separation of power, and compartmentalizing of the resources. Just like in a ship, if the water is infiltrating, you can shut down one unit and still have a backup to buy enough time to fix the problem.

I told you that HR is about managing much human drama and emotions. When all your team is subject to the same core and emotions, it can be dangerous. Do not forget that your team is not the system, it is part of a bigger system with clients and management.

So what you have to realize is that it is your responsibility to keep the entire system running, no matter what. You need backups and redundancies.

This is what I call cheating, with external teams. Many of my companies now operate in hybrid mode between my core team and external components. Sometimes, they are complementing one another. Some other times, they are overlapping, providing security and backups.

To some managers, that is a waste. Not to me. The system is too important and too many people are relying on it to take the chance on one single motor.

So if we redraw the dynamic of the components, there are actually 4 components to your system: the client - the team - the experts consultant, and management. Now your system is more secure.

And as you will be evolving, you will come back to your system and perfect it with more and more components and layers. The key is to balance the forces and to look for sustainability and consistency, no matter what.

To be honest, it is now with that blueprint that I can build a company within days, from an idea to a pilot, to a prototype. I like to build using cells, independent cell structures. I have the minimum team to build the prototype and I buy external expertise for what we lack, branding, legal, marketing, even management.

Then, as I am secure about the chances of success, I will then hire a team. External expertises are expensive at an hourly rate, but if you are smart and run fast, you are paying the hours, not the days and weeks. And this is how I balance my spreadsheet, budget, and risk.

This will bring us to my final advice to you on this journey: Relationships are key! Treat your employees well, treat your partners well, treat your customers well. Your reputation is all that you have.

You wanted a way to cheat?! Here is a great one. **Bet on your credibility**. With a good reputation and good relationship, it is crazy how you can get things done quickly. Often you will benefit from that work even before having completed the full payment of that bill.

But this can only happen as you have cultivated a culture of trust with your networks and contacts. What we often tend to forget is that we are all running against time. Time is costly. Time is scarce. Once gone, it is lost forever. Well, to cheat time, you can do that thanks to your credibility and see how fast people will react to you!

"The most powerful of leverage is when you can borrow time and repay it with the interest you made, borrowing it!"
Dr. BAK NGUYEN

CHEAT SHEET

What I really want you to do is to write down the list of all the people and companies you are dealing with. Now, sort them out as clients, staff, experts, and management. Visualize the system of names you have before your eyes. Now, start to link the dots and see who is working with whom and what is the flow of the operation.

Whatever system you have before your eyes is a mirror of your perspective and personality. If you do not like what you see, feel free to rearrange the dots and the names.

If you like what you are seeing, well, I will invite you to still play with the dots and the names, just to see how it might come out. Now, you are leading and understanding the complexity, the dynamic, and the balance of your system. Oh, and do not forget to look for the ripple effect too!

This is **POWERPLAY, HOW TO BUILD THE PERFECT TEAM.**

There are **employees** and teams.
There are **unions** and ambassadors
There are **liabilities** and assets.
Leverage them well to win.

Dr. BAK NGUYEN

CONCLUSION
BY Dr. BAK NGUYEN

This was my last journey of the year with you. What a year! This was also my first journey with you in the new year, a new year with hope and the promise of a better future.

Well, I am so happy that I took that crazy challenge of mine, waking up yesterday and wanting to flush down 2020 with a world record. I wasn't fast enough to complete this book before the beginning of the new year. Now, it is 7 minutes to midnight, January 1st, 2021. I will have set my latest world record, writing my 78 books within 40 months. What a journey!

I am not only glad because I started the new year with a new world record, but also because I did it, sharing with you a few of my secrets in management and HR. I did not realize how deep I would share with you, and the excitement caught me. I ended up sharing with you most of my tools and edges.

Lay on paper, they might seem just as another opinion, but trust me, it is working. This is how I manage to be as prolific and efficient. Many times, I shared my recipes and mindsets to form momentum. Now I realized that never before, I gave you my tools.

> "My team, mentors and partners are my greatest
> secrets to keep overachieving."
> Dr. BAK NGUYEN

This time you have my blueprint. Hopefully, it will serve you well as you too are walking into the new years and the **New Era of Collaboration**. It was in that spirit that I shared my blueprints and secret, to empower you to leverage and to get to your first wins of the year.

Whenever you will pick up this book, use it wisely, so you are not alone on the path to success. So that you are not alone and running in the hamster wheel, calling it the wheel of fortune.

Yes, some successes will come from luck and chance. But most successes are the result of systems carefully balanced and tuned. This is one of your systems, your team!

Build one, one that you will nurture and empower, one that you can be proud of. One that will elevate you to immortality!

Because to have a team, is to have a system that can be duplicated and perpetuated. And if your system was flexible enough at its core, it may last forever since it can be upgraded!

This is **POWERPLAY, HOW TO BUILD THE PERFECT TEAM.**

There are **employees** and **teams**.
There are **unions** and **ambassadors**
There are **liabilities** and **assets**.
Leverage them well to win.

Dr. BAK NGUYEN

ABOUT THE AUTHORS

From Canada, **Dr. BAK NGUYEN,** Nominee Ernst and Young Entrepreneur of the year, Grand Homage Lys DIVERSITY, LinkedIn & TownHall Achiever of the year and TOP 100 Doctors 2021. Dr Bak is a cosmetic dentist, CEO and founder of Mdex & Co. His company is revolutionizing the dental field. Speaker and motivator, he wrote 72 books over 36 months accumulating many world records (to be officialized).

- **ENTREPRENEURSHIP**
- **LEADERSHIP**
- **QUEST OF IDENTITY**
- **DENTISTRY AND MEDICINE**
- **PARENTING**
- **CHILDREN BOOKS**
- **PHILOSOPHY**

In 2003, he founded Mdex, a dental company upon which in 2018, he launched the most ambitious private endeavour to reform the dental industry, Canada wide. Philosopher, he has close to his heart the quest of happiness of the people surrounding him, patients and colleagues alike. In 2020, he launched an International collaborative initiative named **THE ALPHAS** to share knowledge and for Entrepreneurs and Doctors to thrive through the Greatest Pandemic and Economic depression of our time.

In 2016, he co-found with Tranie Vo, Emotive World Incorporated, a tech research company to use technology to empower happiness and sharing. U.A.X. the ultimate audio experience is the landmark project on which the team is advancing, utilizing the technics of the movie industry and the advancement in ARTIFICIAL INTELLIGENCE to save the book industry and to upgrade the continuing education space.

These projects have allowed Dr Nguyen to attract interests from the international and diplomatic community and he is now the center of a global discussion in the wellbeing and the future of the health profession. It is in that matter that he shares his thoughts and encourages the health community to share their own stories.

"It's not worth it go through it alone! Together, we stand, alone, we fall."

Motivational speaker and serial entrepreneur, philosopher and author, from his own words, Dr Nguyen describes himself as a dentist by circumstances, an entrepreneur by nature and a communicator by passion.

He also holds recognitions from the Canadian Parliament and the Canadian Senate.

www.DrBakNguyen.com

UAX

ULTIMATE AUDIO EXPERIENCE

A new way to learn and enjoy Audiobooks. Made to be entertaining while keeping the self-educational value of a book, UAX will appeal to both auditive and visual people. UAX is the blockbuster of the Audiobooks.

UAX will cover most of Dr Bak's books, and is now negotiating to bring more authors and more titles to the UAX concept. Now streaming on Spotify, Apple Music and available for download on all major music platforms. Give it a try today!

AMAZON - BARNES & NOBLE - APPLE BOOKS - KINDLE
SPOTIFY - APPLE MUSIC

C O M B O
PAPERBACK/AUDIOBOOK
ACTIVATION

Please register your book to receive the link to your audiobook version. Register at: https://baknguyen.com/unicorn-registry

FROM THE SAME AUTHOR
Dr Bak Nguyen

TITLES AVAILABLE AT

www.DrBakNguyen.com

MAJOR LEAGUES' ACCESS

BUSINESS

CHILDREN'S BOOK

with William Bak

The Trilogy of Legends

A TALE OF SPIES AND ALIENS

DENTISTRY

TITLES AVAILABLE AT

www.DrBakNguyen.com

AMAZON - BARNES & NOBLE - APPLE BOOKS - KINDLE
SPOTIFY - APPLE MUSIC

DR.
Bak Nguyen

www.ingramcontent.com/pod-product-compliance
Lightning Source LLC
Chambersburg PA
CBHW061749270326
41928CB00011B/2436